PRIMARY SOURCES OF AMERICAN WARS™

The Spanish-American War

Georgene Poulakidas

The Rosen Publishing Group's
PowerKids Press™
PRIMARY SOURCE

For my brother, Dean

Published in 2006 by The Rosen Publishing Group, Inc.
29 East 21st Street, New York, NY 10010

First Edition

Editor: Eric Fein
Book Design: Erica Clendening
Photo Researcher: Adriana Skura

Photo Credits: Cover © New-York Historical Society, New York, USA/Bridgeman Art Library; p. 4 (left) © Museum of Fine Arts, Houston, Texas, USA, Hogg Brothers Collection, Gift of Miss Ima Hogg/Bridgeman Art Library; pp. 4 (right), 14 © Getty Images; pp. 6 (left), 10 (right), 12 (right), 16 (right), 20 (bottom) © Bettmann/Corbis; p. 6 (right), 12 (left), 18 (right) © Corbis; p. 8 (left) Private Collection, The Stapleton Collection/Bridgeman Art Library; p. 8 American Library, Paris, France Archives Charmet/Bridgeman Art Library; p. 10 (left) © Oscar White/Corbis; p. 16 (left) © North Wind Picture Archives; p. 18 (left) Museo Nazionale (Bargello), Florence, Italy, Index/Bridgeman Art Library; p. 20 (top) © Lake County Museum/Corbis

Library of Congress Cataloging-in-Publication Data

Poulakidas, Georgene.
    The Spanish-American War / Georgene Poulakidas.— 1st ed.
    p. cm. — (Primary sources of American wars)
    Includes bibliographical references and index.
    ISBN 1-4042-2685-0 (lib. bdg.)
    1. Spanish-American War, 1898—Juvenile literature. I. Title. II. Series.

    E715.P68 2006
    973.8'9—dc22

                                                        2004001253

Manufactured in the United States of America

Contents

1 Revolution in Cuba — 5

2 Angry Americans — 7

3 "Remember the *Maine!*" — 9

4 The Battle of Manila Bay — 11

5 The Cuban Blockade — 13

6 Teddy Roosevelt and the Rough Riders — 15

7 Harbor of Death — 17

8 The War's End — 19

9 Results of the War — 21

Timeline — 22

Glossary — 23

Index — 24

Primary Sources — 24

Web Sites — 24

This painting by American artist Frederic Remington shows a U.S. soldier at the time of the Spanish-American War. The average age of an American soldier who fought in the war was twenty-seven years.

Revolution in Cuba

The Spanish-American War was fought from April 1898 to August 1898. This brief war between the United States and Spain grew out of Cuba's struggle for independence. Spain was a **colonial** power in the late nineteenth century. Spain controlled Cuba and Puerto Rico in Latin America, the Philippine Islands and Guam in the Pacific Ocean, and other nations as well.

Spain did not allow the Cuban people to govern themselves, nor did they allow the Cubans many personal liberties. This angered the people of Cuba. From 1868 to 1878, many Cubans **revolted** against Spain in the Ten Years' War. Tens of thousands of Spanish soldiers were sent to Cuba to stop the **rebellion**. Over 200,000 people died during this revolt. Many people in the United States were angered by Spanish **brutality** against the Cubans.

■ *In this photo, rebel Cuban soldiers are shown cooking a pig for dinner. Spain's harsh treatment of Cuban citizens angered many Americans. This set the stage for conflict between Spain and the United States.*

5

■ Joseph Pulitzer (1847–1911) was a politician and the owner and publisher of the New York World. In his newspaper, Pulitzer urged the United States to go to war with Spain. The World was also the first American newspaper to have a comic strip section.

Angry Americans

In 1895, Cuba once again revolted against Spain. Spain then sent more than 100,000 troops into Cuba. These troops were led by General Valeriano Weyler y Nicolau. Weyler was called the Butcher because he treated the Cubans so poorly. He sent thousands of people into prison camps, where they died from hunger and illness.

Many Americans were angry at Spain's actions. Their feelings grew even stronger after reading the reports of these actions in American newspapers such as the *New York Journal* and the *New York World*. The newspapers also encouraged the United States to go to war with Spain to protect the Cubans. Many Americans thought that a **victory** over Spain would also help establish the United States as a true world power.

■ *General Valeriano Weyler y Nicolau (1838–1890) was named governor of Cuba in 1896 to help stop the Cuban rebellion. His actions resulted in the death of thousands of Cubans due to hunger and disease.*

President William McKinley (1843–1901) was the twenty-fifth president of the United States, serving from 1897 to 1901. Even after the destruction of the Maine, McKinley tried to find a peaceful solution to the question of Cuba's independence.

"Remember the *Maine!*"

In January 1898, **rioting** broke out in Havana, Cuba. To protect Americans living in the city, the United States sent the U.S.S. *Maine*, a warship, to Havana. The ship stayed in Havana's harbor. On February 15, an underwater **explosion** rocked the *Maine*. This explosion sank the ship and killed about 266 American sailors on board.

Many Americans believed that the Spanish government was responsible for the sinking of the *Maine*. "Remember the *Maine!*" became America's battle cry. Although there was no strong proof that Spain was involved in the sinking, support for a war grew. However, President William McKinley was not ready to go to war. He sent letters to Spain ordering that Cuba be given its independence. Spain refused, but agreed to calm the fighting in Cuba. Spain's offer was too little, too late.

■ *This photo shows the wreckage of the battleship USS Maine. The ship remained sunk in Havana's harbor until 1910. It was refloated and brought to the Gulf of Mexico, where it was sunk with military honors and ceremonies.*

■ Admiral George Dewey (1837–1917) became a war hero following his victory over the Spanish navy at Manila Bay. Earlier in his career, Dewey had served with the Union navy during the American Civil War.

The Battle of Manila Bay

On April 25, 1898, the United States officially **declared** war against Spain. Its first military action was to attack the Philippines and Guam, about 9,000 miles (14,484 km) from the United States.

On May 1, U.S. Navy commander George Dewey sailed into Manila Bay in the Philippines with six battleships. Dewey's orders were to destroy the Spanish navy that was based there. Dewey and his ships had been stationed in nearby Hong Kong since late 1897, ready to attack the Philippines if the United States declared war. In about six hours, Dewey destroyed all 10 Spanish ships in Manila Bay. About 160 Spanish sailors were killed and 210 were hurt during the battle. No American sailors were killed and only a few were hurt. Dewey then set up a **blockade** of the harbor while he waited for U.S. ground troops to arrive.

■ *This painting shows American ships in action at the Battle of Manila Bay. In about six hours, American warships sunk or captured the entire Spanish fleet of the Pacific Ocean.*

Rear Admiral William T. Sampson (1840–1902) was commander of the American blockade that pinned in the Spanish navy at the harbor of Santiago de Cuba. Four American warships have been named USS Sampson in his honor.

The Cuban Blockade

In late May, U.S. naval ships, under the command of Rear Admiral William T. Sampson, set up a blockade of the harbor of Santiago de Cuba, in southeastern Cuba. This trapped the Spanish navy, led by Admiral Pascual Cervera y Topete, in the harbor. Meanwhile, the U.S. Army prepared to attack the island by land.

By late June, American forces gathered in large numbers off Santiago de Cuba. The United States now had 153 ships and about 16,200 soldiers ready for battle. Major General William R. Shafter was in charge of the ground forces. On June 22, 15,000 soldiers landed near Santiago, at Daiquiri and Siboney. Among these troops were Teddy Roosevelt and the Rough Riders.

■ *In this photo taken in about April 1898, American troops land on a beach in Cuba.*

Theodore Roosevelt (1858–1919) was a colonel in the U.S. volunteer army when he fought at the Battle of San Juan Hill. Roosevelt was the twenty-sixth president of the United States.

14

Teddy Roosevelt and the Rough Riders

On June 24, 1898, Roosevelt led his Rough Riders into the Battle of Las Guasimas. This was the first land battle of the war. Although the Spanish had a stronger force, the Rough Riders chased them from their positions.

On July 1, the Rough Riders took part in the Battle of San Juan Hill. Roosevelt led his men on a charge up Kettle Hill, near San Juan Hill. They were attacking Spanish forces at the top of the hill. During the fighting, 15 of Roosevelt's men were killed and 76 were hurt. Although the Americans won the battle, it came at a heavy price. Overall, over 280 U.S. soldiers were killed and more than 1,500 were hurt. The U.S. commanders were shocked by these heavy losses, and they failed to follow up on their victory.

■ *This photo shows the Rough Riders, Theodore Roosevelt's army unit, on board a ship at Tampa, Florida. The Rough Riders sailed from Tampa to Santiago de Cuba in mid-June 1898.*

■ In this drawing (above), Spanish admiral Pascual Cervera (dark suit) is being taken prisoner aboard the USS Iowa, following his defeat at the battle in Santiago harbor.

YOUR COUNTRY CALLS YOU

R·M·WRIG
'98

Harbor of Death

The officer in charge of Spain's forces was also shaken by the July 1 battle. He believed that Spain could not hold onto Santiago de Cuba. He ordered Admiral Cervera to move his ships to sea so they would not be captured by the United States. This would prove to be a big mistake. On July 3, 1898, Cervera led the Spanish ships out of the harbor. They went one at a time because the harbor was very narrow. Cervera had seven ships under his command. Each one was destroyed or driven to the shore by gunfire from the U.S. ships. This attack lasted only a few hours. The Spanish suffered 323 deaths and 151 wounded in the battle. The Americans had one person killed and one hurt. The Americans took Cervera and over 1,700 Spanish troops as prisoners.

■ *Posters such as this one (left) were used during the Spanish-American War to urge American men to join the armed forces.*

The American flag was raised above the governor's palace after the American victory at Santiago de Cuba. The city was founded in 1514.

The War's End

After the sea battle at Santiago de Cuba, the war quickly came to an end. After days of talks, Spanish forces in Santiago **surrendered** on July 17, 1898. On July 25, U.S. forces led by General Nelson A. Miles took control of Puerto Rico. Back in the Philippines, U.S. forces gained control of the city of Manila on August 13.

The United States and Spain signed a peace **treaty** on December 10, 1898, in Paris, France. The treaty called for Spain to grant Cuba its freedom. Spain was also forced to give up Guam, Puerto Rico, and the Philippines to the United States. In return, the United States paid Spain $20 million for the Philippines. The treaty was officially approved by the U.S. Congress on February 6, 1899—by just one vote.

■ *In this photo, joyous American soldiers celebrate the news of Spain's surrender of Santiago de Cuba.*

This photo (left) shows the building of the Panama Canal. The canal allows for a quick route from the Atlantic Ocean to the Pacific Ocean. It cuts through the Central American country of Panama.

20

Results of the War

The Spanish-American War marked the end of Spain's colonial power. It also established the United States as an important worldwide military force. The war showed the importance of having a strong navy positioned around the world. America's win helped speed the construction of the Panama Canal, which was completed in 1914. This **canal** linked the Atlantic Ocean to the Pacific Ocean, which allowed for faster travel for U.S. business and military operations. The land Cuba gave to the United States included Guantánamo Bay. This area became an important base for the U.S. Navy for many years. War hero Theodore Roosevelt went on to become president of the United States in 1901. These important results make the Spanish-American War an important part of U.S. history.

■ *Guantánamo Bay, Cuba, is the home of a U.S. naval station. The station is the only U.S. base in operation in a Communist nation.*

Timeline

1868–1878, 1895	Cubans rebel against Spain. Spain defeats both rebellions.
January 1898	Disorder breaks out in Havana, Cuba. The U.S.S. *Maine* is sent to Havana to protect Americans.
February 15, 1898	The U.S.S. *Maine* is sunk by an explosion.
April 25, 1898	The United States officially declares war on Spain.
May 1, 1898	The Battle of Manila Bay is fought.
Late May 1898	U.S. Navy blockades the harbor of Santiago de Cuba.
June 22, 1898	Fifteen thousand U.S. soldiers land near Santiago de Cuba.
June 24, 1898	The Battle of Las Guasimas is fought.
July 1, 1898	The Battle of San Juan Hill is fought.
July 3, 1898	U.S. naval ships destroy or put to shore seven Spanish ships as they try to escape the harbor of Santiago de Cuba.
July 17, 1898	Spanish forces in Santiago surrender.
July 25, 1898	U.S. forces invade Puerto Rico.
August 13, 1898	U.S. forces take control of Manila, bringing the war to an end.
December 10, 1898	A peace treaty is signed by the United States and Spain.
February 6, 1899	The treaty is officially approved by the U.S. Congress.

Glossary

blockade (blok-ADE) A closing off of an area to keep people or supplies from going in or out.

brutality (broo-TAL-ih-tee) Cruel and violent actions.

canal (kuh-NAL) A channel that is dug across land. Canals connect bodies of water so that ships can travel between them.

colonial (kuh-LOH-nee-uhl) Having to do with territory that has been settled by people from another country and is controlled by that country.

declared (di-KLAIRD) To have announced something formally.

explosion (ek-SPLOH-zhuhn) A sudden and noisy release of energy.

rebellion (ri-BEL-yuhn) An armed fight against a government, or any struggle against the people in charge of something.

revolted (ri-VOHLT-ihd) To have fought against authority.

rioting (RYE-uht-ihng) Behaving in a noisy, violent, and usually uncontrollable way.

surrendered (suh-REN-durd) To have given up, or admitted that you are beaten in a fight or battle.

treaty (TREE-tee) A formal agreement between two or more countries.

victory (VIK-tuh-ree) A win in a battle or contest.

Index

B
Battle of San Juan
   Hill, 15
blockade, 11, 13
brutality, 5

C
canal, 21
colonial, 5, 21
Cuba, 5, 7, 9, 13,
   17, 19, 21

D
declared, 11
Dewey, George,
   11

E
explosion, 9

M
Manila Bay, 11
McKinley, William,
   9

P
Philippines, 11, 19
Puerto Rico, 5, 19

R
rebellion, 5
revolted, 5, 7

rioting, 9
Roosevelt, Teddy,
   13, 15, 21
Rough Riders, 13,
   15

S
Sampson, William,
   13
Santiago de Cuba,
   13, 17, 19
Spain, 5, 7, 9, 11,
   17, 19, 21
surrendered, 19

T
treaty, 19

U
U.S.S. *Maine*, 9

V
victory, 7, 15

Primary Sources

Cover: *Destruction of the U.S. battleship* Maine *in Havana Harbor, February 15, 1898.* Color lithograph by Kurz and Allison. New-York Historical Society. **Page Four (inset):** *U.S. Soldier, Spanish American War (A First-Class Fighting Man).* Oil on canvas by Frederic Remington [1899]. Museum of Fine Arts, Houston, Texas. **Page Four:** Rebel soldiers in Cuba. "The Insurrection in Cuba." Published in the *Illustrated London News* [1896]. **Page Six (left):** Photograph of Joseph Pulitzer [Date unknown]. Bettmann/Corbis. **Page Six (right):** Photograph of General Valeriano Weyler y Nicolau, Marques Tenerife [late nineteenth century]. Corbis. **Page 8 (inset):** Portrait of William McKinley. Lithograph by American School [date unknown]. The Stapleton Collection. **Page 8:** *The Catastrophe of the USS Maine, 1898.* Photograph. American Library, Paris, France. Archives Charmet. **Page 10 (inset):** Photograph of Admiral George Dewey. Oscar White, photographer [date unknown]. Oscar White/Corbis. **Page 10:** *The Spanish-American War: U.S. fleet desroying the Spanish fleet at Manila, May, 1898.* Lithograph [c. 1898]. Bettmann/Corbis. **Page 12 (inset):** Photograph of Rear Admiral William Thomas Sampson [c. 1890s]. Corbis. **Page 12:** *The first American troops land on a beach in Cuba at the start of the Spanish-American War.* Photograph [c. April 1898]. Bettmann/Corbis. **Page 14 (inset):** Theodore Roosevelt in the uniform of a lieutenant-colonel of the Rough Riders. Photograph by Rockwood [c. 1898]. Hulton Archive. **Page 14:** Rough Riders leaving aboard the ship *Concho*, Tampa, Florida. Photograph [1898]. Hulton Archive. **Page 16 (left):** Spanish admiral Cervera taken aboard the USS *Iowa*, Battle of Santiago, 1898. Hand-colored halftone [c. 1898]. North Wind Picture Archives. **Page 16 (right):** War recruitment poster with flag and bugler [c. 1898]. Bettmann/Corbis. **Page 18 (inset):** The Surrender of Santiago de Cuba. Engraved by Tilly, engraving by Spanish School [c. 1898]. Museo Nazionale (Bargello), Florence, Italy. Bridgeman Art Library. **Page 18:** Receiving the news of surrender of Santiago, Cuba, 1898. Photograph by Scribners Collection [1898]. Corbis. **Page 20 (inset):** Panama Canal under construction. Photograph [c. 1913]. Lake County Museum/Corbis. **Page 20:** U.S. air base at Guantánamo Bay, Cuba. Photograph [1988]. Bettmann/Corbis.

Web Sites

Due to the changing nature of Internet links, PowerKids Press has developed an online list of Web sites related to the topic of this book. This site is updated regularly. Please use this link to access the list:
http://www.powerkidslinks.com/psaw/saw/